CLASSIC ROCK

Arranged by Chad Johnson

ISBN 978-1-4768-2304-1

HAL•LEONARD®
CORPORATION
7777 W. BLUEMOUND RD. P.O. BOX 13819 MILWAUKEE, WI 53213

Visit Hal Leonard Online at
www.halleonard.com

Aqualung

Words and Music by Ian Anderson and Jennie Anderson

Behind Blue Eyes

Words and Music by Peter Townshend

Born to Be Wild

Words and Music by Mars Bonfire

Crazy Train

Words and Music by Ozzy Osbourne, Randy Rhoads and Bob Daisley

Fly Like an Eagle

Words and Music by Steve Miller

Free Bird

Words and Music by Allen Collins and Ronnie Van Zant

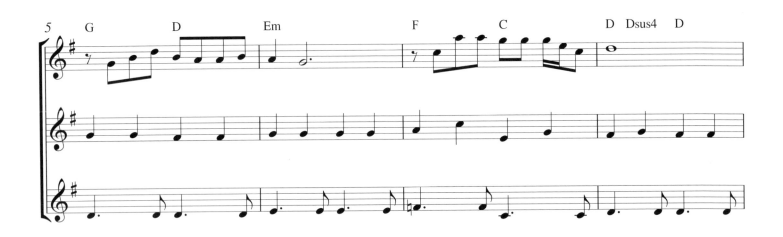

Hey Jude

Words and Music by John Lennon and Paul McCartney

Low Rider

Words and Music by Sylvester Allen, Harold R. Brown, Morris Dickerson,
Jerry Goldstein, Leroy Jordan, Lee Oskar, Charles W. Miller and Howard Scott

Moondance

Words and Music by Van Morrison

Oye Como Va

Words and Music by Tito Puente

Proud Mary

Words and Music by John Fogerty

(I Can't Get No)
Satisfaction

Words and Music by Mick Jagger and Keith Richards

Smoke on the Water

Words and Music by Ritchie Blackmore, Ian Gillan,
Roger Glover, Jon Lord and Ian Paice

Summertime Blues

Words and Music by Eddie Cochran and Jerry Capehart

Sunshine of Your Love

Words and Music by Jack Bruce, Pete Brown and Eric Clapton

NOTES FROM THE ARRANGER

Arranging for three ukuleles can be challenging because of the instrument's limited range. In standard tuning (G-C-E-A), there is only one octave plus a major sixth between the open C string and fret 12 on the A string. Certain melodies easily span this distance and more, so compromises sometimes had to be made.

Not all ukuleles have the same number of frets. If your uke has fewer than 15 frets, you may need to play certain phrases an octave lower (especially in Part I). Some phrases have already been transposed up or down an octave—this was only done out of necessity and kept to a minimum. A few songs require every inch of available fretboard, but fret 15 on the first string (high C) is the limit, and this is extremely rare.

The three voices will sometimes cross as a result of range limitations. If Part III is considered to be the "bass" line, keep in mind that the lowest available "bass" notes are sometimes on the first string! However, if you own a baritone ukulele, almost all of the notes in Part III could be played an octave lower (except the open C string and C♯ on fret 1), thus providing a more effective bass line.

Despite the above caveats, I believe that the spirit of these songs has been preserved, and I hope you enjoy playing these arrangements as much as I enjoyed creating them. By the way, a fourth ensemble part can be added by strumming along with the chord symbols!

– Chad Johnson

SOPRANO, CONCERT & TENOR FRETBOARD

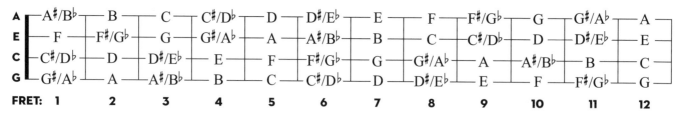

BARITONE FRETBOARD

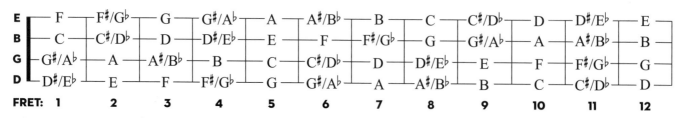